Made in Tomorrow

Katherine Myers

Presentation by *BookLeaf Publishing*

Web: www.bookleafpub.com

E-mail: info@bookleafpub.com

ISBN: 9789357740388

First edition 2023

For the former me, who has changed so much in life.

And for my Grandparents, Nick and Katelyn a.k.a Agent Z

ACKNOWLEDGEMENT

Firstly thanks to my boyfriend, Nick, for helping me keep this project a secret from our friends and my family.

Thank you to Katelyn, my best friend, and the fact you have always supported my writing.

Lastly, I would like to thank my grandparents for their support of my dream even as it changes amongst genres.

Comfort of Time

The possibility of comfort
is the essentiality of time,
kissing the soul of man

A dare to peace in life
whether a lie or truth
peace is a piece of the puzzle

Till the truth of death,
the comfort of time

A Space in the Night

A place where moonlit flowers
grow and sparkle.
Where moonlight pools,
for those who wander.
A home of inspiration,
for the people of the night.

To a Memory

3

Some days you wish
to go back to a
place in your memories

To a place long forgotten

To a place with beautiful beaches

To a place of firsts

Some days you just wish for escapes

Time is Ticking

Ding-dong
The clock strikes the hour.
Not a thing's been done.
Ding-dong
What happens now,
with time passing
No questions asked.
Ding-dong
How do we get through this
Where can we go now?
Silence the clock has finished.
Back to doing nothing, or
perhaps
I should work on something now,
After all,
time is not infinite.

Missing You

I miss you,

I love you,

but no matter what

I can't remember you

The more I grow,
the more I wish I still had you.

Search

Everyone is searching for something
...a place
...a person
...a thing
...a feeling
but it is always something.

Some find it quickly,
some let it find them,
and others search and search without luck

but eventually, it will find you,
and who knows if you even knew exactly what
you were looking for.

Shattered

Fragile as a glass
    impacts
crack and chip

Eventually, it'll shatter

The pieces broken are hard to mend.

We are but a piece of the glass we once were.

Looking Through

I look through the keyhole
to see the locked world beyond.
A world of dreams,
with tall castles
and more colors than can be seen.

The World of Dreams
some may call it,
but all people dream
and there is no key

Possibility of a Kiss

9

Sunshine and rain
kiss to make,
a world of rainbow

A whisper of daring possibility
about man in time,
beauty made of opposites

A Pawprint

Proof that you lived
moved and mattered.

Beautiful stories they hold
and messes
they made

Time changed them
They fade from
the places they were left

But hold firm like claws
on the heart

Paws walk
beside feet
even after life.

untitled

each world could

bloom of ecstatic whispers

between the souls

who would shine

Whispers

between the warmth of life
there are moments
after last heart
whispering of happiness

Walk in Darkness

13

Walk amongst the streets
of darkened houses.
In search of treats.
Quiet as a mouse.

The windows lit
where people work
in preference of areas un-sunlit,
especially those that do artwork.

Walking the Line

barefoot
in
the
blue sky

a
last
moment

between
life

and
a
dream

Hidden

15

You are "perfect", the golden child...
I am average.

The world bends over backward for you...
it suffocates me.

The universe blesses you...
it curses me.

The world showers you in light...
it hides me in darkness.

Lost in Time

Life stops
Yet time goes on
Time stops
Life continues
Time and Life
Unconnected yet connected
Every moment focused on the time,
Life slips by again.
Push and pull,
they go.
"Go together" we beg
let life and time move
as a whole.
Time goes on and we
lose life in the maze.
Can life go on in lost time?
Can life go on lost in time?
No one can truly know the answers.

Song of Light

17

  if light
is the warmth
in the moment

song of heart
sings comfort
   between
world and wonder

Seasons

Four Seasons
Winter, Spring, Summer, and Fall.
Ice and snow
wind like needless
melt in the sun, a sign of
Spring as birds
return home.
With sun and rain the
trees bring the shade of
Summer.
Soon leaves change in color
Red, yellow, and orange
fall from the trees as the seasons change.
Time passes still and cold sets in
as snow makes for igloos
of Winter.
The seasons pass to come again year after year.

Creatures

Built with claws and wings,

teeth that kill, and

horns that can grant wishes.

Creatures people know,
as well as the new.

Fiction and fantasy
or a part of reality.

Waiting

Enjoy a happy wonder,
from a dream.

Living in a world
of whispers in time.

A soul said
'dare comfort for joy always comes'

Soon too for
you dreamer

When Tomorrow Comes

Tomorrow will come

Even if the world gets destroyed,
it will come.

Even if we are not here,
Tomorrow will come.

We can never be ready for what comes with it,
but tomorrow always comes.

Tomorrow is what it will be and it always comes
even if we will
the tomorrows to slow, we will live and they will
come.

Till tomorrow.

9 789357 740388